Page
The beginning of the story	-	-	-	4
Measuring time by the moon	-	-	-	6
Measuring time by shadows	-	-	-	8
The beginnings of astronomy	-	-	-	10
The importance of fire	-	-	-	12
Early medical beliefs	-	-	-	14
New civilisations	-	-	-	16
New civilisations (continued)	-	-	-	18
The Ancient Greeks	-	-	-	20
Early physics – the basic elements	-	-	22
Greek medicine and biology	-	-	24
Science moves to Alexandria	-	-	-	26
Euclid and Archimedes	-	-	-	28
Measuring the world	-	-	-	30
Ptolemy – astronomer and map maker	-	-	32
Science in Rome and China	-	-	-	34
Chemistry	-	-	-	36
Science reaches the West	-	-	-	38
Improvements in navigation	-	-	-	40
A changing world	-	-	-	42
Leonardo da Vinci	-	-	-	44
The new astronomy	-	-	-	46
Changing ideas on the universe	-	-	48
Galileo and the telescope	-	-	-	50

Ladybird books recommended for further reading on subjects mentioned in this book:

Series 601

> Great Inventions
> Exploring Space
> The Story of Printing
> The Story of Metals
> The Story of Medicine
> Time, Calendars and Clocks

Series 561

> Stone Age Man in Britain
> Christopher Columbus
> Alexander the Great
> Great Civilisations—Egypt

Series 536

> The Night Sky

Series 654

> How it works—The Telescope and Microscope
> How it works—Printing Processes

Series 701

> Great Artists   Book 2—Leonardo da Vinci

The publishers wish to acknowledge the advice and assistance of A. P. Sanday, M.A., Science Adviser, Warwickshire, L.E.A., when preparing this book.

Book 1

The story of
Science

by EDMUND HUNTER

with illustrations
by B. H. ROBINSON

Publishers: Ladybird Books Ltd . Loughborough
© Ladybird Books Ltd 1973
Printed in England

The beginning of the story

The story of science is the story of Man's efforts to understand himself and the mysterious universe around him. Perhaps it is really two stories because science has two main parts. One is the study of all natural things and might be called the search for knowledge. The other deals with the use that Man has been able to make of the earth's resources and the gradual development of man-made instruments, machines and materials. We could call this the science of technology.

It is believed that the earth's crust was formed more than a thousand million years ago. Early Man probably made his appearance about two million years ago; but it was not until about 7000 BC that people began to live in villages, cultivating plants for food and tending animals such as sheep and goats. The arts of painting and carving were being developed, and it is certain that there was great interest in the surrounding lands and in the sun, moon and stars.

Man noticed how the sun brought light and warmth, how the stars appeared after dark, sometimes with the moon and sometimes without it. He noticed how the moon regularly changed its shape over the same period of time.

0 7214 0353 0

Arrow and Lance Heads

Stone Hammer

Clay Sickle

Mattock

Fish Hooks

Part of a rock painting discovered in the Sahara, which was a fertile region in prehistoric times

Measuring time by the moon

The appearance of a new moon at intervals of about twenty-nine days gave our early ancestors a convenient method of measuring time. For this reason the first calendar was a lunar (moon) one and the year was made up of twelve 'moons'.

The lunar calendar was helpful in some ways, but took no account of the seasons. For people who relied on agriculture for their living, this was a serious matter. The period from new moon to new moon is not exactly twenty-nine days, it is nearer twenty-nine and a half. But even that figure is not entirely accurate. As a result, each lunar calendar year was short by at least eleven days ($12 \times 29\frac{1}{2} = 354$) and in three years the calendar was more than thirty days (a whole month) out of step with the seasons.

As time went by, Man began to realise that the sun provided a more accurate measurement of time. It rose each morning and set each evening, giving periods of day and night. Man also began to notice that the height of the sun in the sky differed according to the time of year.

Above: The moon's phases, with outer circle showing the changes viewed from space and the inner circle showing how we see them from earth.
Below: Four stages in the earth's cycle each year.

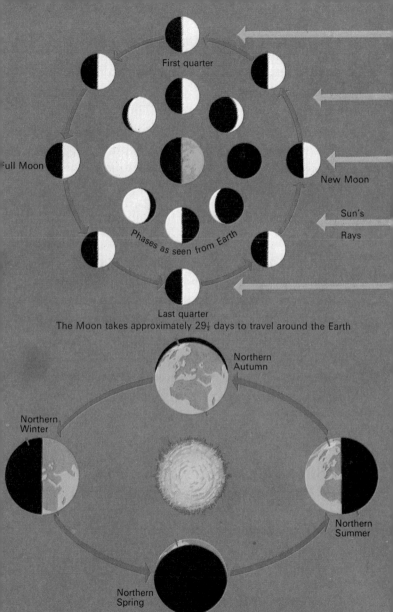

First quarter

Full Moon

New Moon

Sun's

Rays

Phases as seen from Earth

Last quarter

The Moon takes approximately 29½ days to travel around the Earth

Northern
Autumn

Northern
Winter

Northern
Summer

Northern
Spring

The Earth takes 365¼ days to travel around the Sun

Measuring time by shadows

Seven thousand years ago, people had no previous information to guide them. Everything had to be learned from observation and experience. Thus, what we take for granted, they had to work out painstakingly over a great number of years. Therefore, having discovered that the height of the sun varied at different times of the year, Man had still to discover the relationship of this to the seasons.

The length of the shadow of a stake in the ground varies during the day, and is shortest at mid-day – that is, half-way between sunrise and sunset. At mid-day during the cold season of the year, it was noticed that the sun was much lower in the sky than at mid-day in the warm season. The lower the position of the sun at mid-day the longer were the shadows cast by objects on the ground. The higher the sun, the shorter were the shadows. By measuring the varying lengths of a particular shadow at mid-day a reasonably accurate idea of the seasons could be gained.

Early man drove a stake into the ground and measured the length of the shadow it cast at mid-day at various times of the year. A stake used for this purpose was the earliest type of sundial and was called a *gnomon*. It is interesting that some primitive peoples still use this same method.

At the same time of day, shadows are longer in winter than in summer.

A Borneo tribesman measures the shadow of a gnomon

The beginnings of astronomy

Early men were also greatly interested in the stars they saw twinkling in the sky at night. What they did not realise was that the stars were also present during the daytime, but their light was not visible because of the brilliance of the sun. How did they discover this?

There is one event which does enable us to see the stars in the daytime. It is the total eclipse of the sun, when the moon passes in front of the sun and hides it from view. When this happens, the sky becomes dark enough for the stars to be seen. Total eclipses of this kind do not occur very often and are not likely to be seen from the same area more than once every fifty-four years. One can imagine what an awe-inspiring sight it must have been for an early man, who would remember the event for the rest of his life.

So Man watched the movements of the sun, the moon and the stars and wondered about them. In thinking about what they were and what they did he was practising the oldest branch of science – astronomy.

Early Man watches a total eclipse of the sun. We know now that this can damage one's eyes unless special precautions are taken.

The importance of fire

The study of 'heavenly bodies' was only a very small part of Man's activities in those distant days. He lived in primitive conditions, and anything that could make life a little easier or more bearable interested him.

It is not known with any certainty when man first learned how to make use of fire, but when he did his life was changed in many ways. With fire he found he had a means of keeping warm in cold weather, of boiling water, cooking meals and frightening away wild animals. Later, he found that fire (together with charcoal) could be used to extract certain metals from ores. Then he shaped metals into tools, weapons and ornaments. Later still, it was found that two metals together could form a stronger *alloy*.* The mixing of copper and tin, for instance, produces bronze, a much-used metal for many centuries. Thus the science of metallurgy began, although it came about more by chance than by any planned aim on the part of those engaged in it.

Today, we realise that flames are produced by burning gases, but to early Man fire was a complete mystery. He thought of it as a basic element, a gift of nature, something even to be worshipped like a god.

* See the Ladybird book 'The Story of Metals'.

Bronze-casters at work — about 1500 BC, and a selection of bronze implements.

Open stone-mould
for an axe

Two halves of a
closed clay mould

Furnace with goat-skin bellows in use

Pouring molten bronze
into a mould

Mould supported in pile of sand

Spearhead

Hammer

Chisel

Razor

Reaping
Hook

Brooch

Early medical beliefs

The average life-span of our early ancestors was little more than thirty to forty years. People suffered from many diseases caused by the conditions in which they lived. Battles with neighbouring tribes, and attacks by wild animals, were added dangers. It was natural, therefore, that much thought should be given to the problems of curing the sick and injured.

It was discovered that when a person stopped breathing, death followed immediately and the flow of blood ceased. Why this happened was not known but it was generally believed that the blood was some sort of magical 'life spirit'. Indeed, magic and medicine were closely connected, the mystic rituals of the medicine man being considered just as important as the taking of potions, plant juices and herbs.

Operations were performed even in those early times, and the most surprising of these was *trepanning*. In this operation, which is still carried out today, a hole is cut in the patient's skull. The modern version of this process helps to relieve pressure on the brain; the crude, though occasionally successful, trepanning of thousands of years ago was probably carried out because it was thought that this released an evil spirit from the poor patient's head.

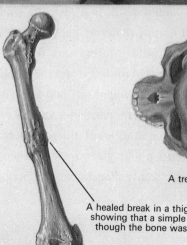

A trepanned skull

A healed break in a thighbone
showing that a simple splint was used
though the bone was not properly set

New civilisations

Generation followed generation and, as the centuries passed, new civilisations were formed. People began to live in much larger communities, cities were built and life became more complicated. Although nomadic tribes continued to wander from area to area, more people tended to settle down with others of similar race, thought and interest. National characteristics developed and trade grew.

By the year 3000 BC, the great civilisations of Egypt and Sumer (later Babylonia) were flourishing in the Middle East. It was here that early scientific thought and practice continued to progress for the next two thousand five hundred years.

People learned how to use levers and rollers to move heavy objects. They invented a form of writing and found a way of making a writing material, papyrus, from rushes which grew by the Nile. Mining was well organised and smelting was carried on to extract the metal from ore-bearing rock. Glass-making flourished as early as 1350 BC. Beads and vases were made in a variety of colours by blending-in small quantities of different metal compounds. The Egyptians could glaze their earthenware utensils, dye fabrics, weave fine linen and make beautiful articles of gold.

A Sumerian city and temple

Egyptian statue
of a scribe

The Egyptians used levers and rollers
to move the massive blocks of stone
to build the pyramids

Egyptian hieroglyphics

Medical knowledge was slowly being gathered. The Egyptians knew that damage to the brain could cause other parts of the body to become paralysed. They were experts at preserving the bodies of the dead by embalming them with special lotions and juices. Today, after three thousand years, Egyptian 'mummies' can still be seen in our museums.

The Babylonians were also a practical people but were more interested than the Egyptians in finding out *why* things happened. They were, in fact, the first people to produce scientific theories. They, too, were able to write, using slabs of clay as the writing material. In mathematics they were able to work out the squares and square roots of numbers. They counted in sixties as well as in tens, and we still use their 'sixty' system in the 360° measurement of a circle and in sixty-second and sixty-minute units of time.

To the Babylonians the earth was flat and set in a vast area of sea. This seemed logical to them because if they travelled far enough overland in any direction, they always came to the sea. They thought of the sky as a huge dome made of some sort of material, supported all round by high mountains rising out of the sea.

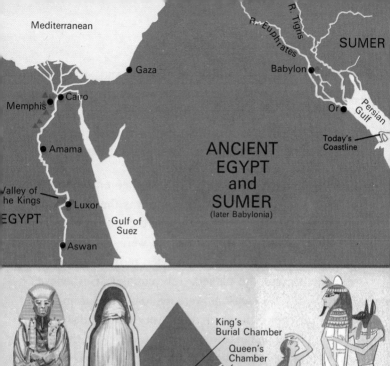

Mediterranean

SUMER

R. Euphrates
R. Tigris

Gaza

Babylon

Cairo

Memphis

Or

Persian
Gulf

Amama

Today's
Coastline

ANCIENT
EGYPT
and
SUMER
(later Babylonia)

Valley of
the Kings

Luxor

EGYPT

Gulf of
Suez

Aswan

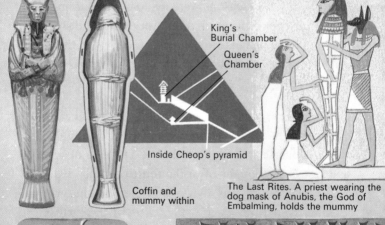

King's
Burial Chamber

Queen's
Chamber

Inside Cheop's pyramid

Coffin and
mummy within

The Last Rites. A priest wearing the
dog mask of Anubis, the God of
Embalming, holds the mummy

Earliest known form of picture writing from Sumer,
and cuneiform script which developed from it

The Ancient Greeks

While the civilisations of Egypt and Babylonia flourished, other Middle Eastern states were developing. Of these, Greece is the most important to our story of science. It was the home of great scientists and philosophers such as Pythagoras, Aristotle and Plato.

Pythagoras is best known for his theorem about the sides of a right-angled triangle. He was the first person to believe that the earth was a sphere. Some of his other scientific ideas, while not correct were yet important steps forward. He thought that the movements of the sun, moon and the planets were circular. He believed that the different seasons were made by the sun moving in a circle round the earth once every year, and that the moon and the planets moved round the earth in the same way. He believed that the earth was thus the centre of the universe.

Aristotle also accepted the idea of a spherical earth as the central body with a fixed position, and thought the whole universe to be spherical also. The idea of *gravity* had not been thought of in the fourth century BC, but Aristotle's theory was that a body fell to the ground seeking its 'natural place' – the centre of the earth.

(Right above)   Although the Egyptians may have known for a long time how to make a right angle, it is probable that Pythagoras was the first to prove that the square on the hypotenuse of a right-angled triangle is equal to the sum of the squares on the other two sides.

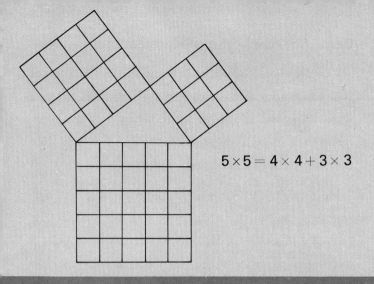

$$5 \times 5 = 4 \times 4 + 3 \times 3$$

It was thought that the Earth was at the centre of a system of transparent crystal spheres, attached to which were the sun, moon, planets and stars. The diagram shows the imaginary spheres cut in half

Early physics – the basic elements

The Greek philosophers believed in the existence of four basic substances or elements – earth, air, fire and water. Aristotle added the idea that each of these elements had its natural place in the universe, and that everything else was made up of them.

He thought that air was contained in a sphere surrounding the earth, which was why air was always around and about us. He noticed that whichever way a burning object was turned, the flame always travelled upwards – so he thought that fire must be contained in a sphere above the air and the flame was trying to reach its natural place there. When water was poured, he noticed that it spread over the ground, so he thought that the natural place for it was down on the earth. Finally he thought that the remaining element, earth, had its place as the centre of the universe. It was believed that everything was composed of all four elements in different proportions.

So Man continued to find theories to account for the nature of the universe around him. It is not important that these theories turned out to be incorrect. They laid the foundation for future thought and discovery.

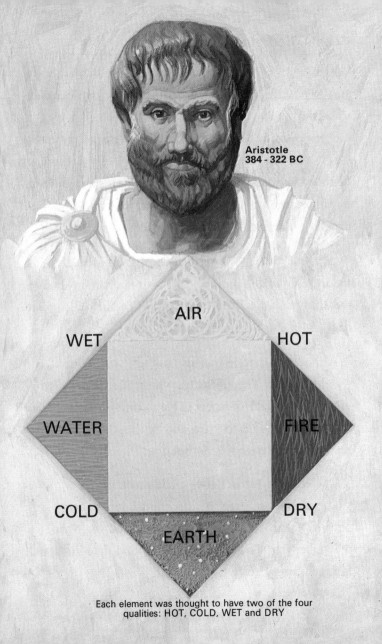

Aristotle
384 - 322 BC

AIR

WET

HOT

WATER

FIRE

COLD

DRY

EARTH

Each element was thought to have two of the four
qualities: HOT, COLD, WET and DRY

Greek medicine and biology

The Greeks were great observers of the human body and of nature. Most famous of the Greek medical men was Hippocrates who is chiefly remembered today for the 'Hippocratic Oath'. This oath is a series of promises that some doctors still make before they become qualified to practise their profession. Hippocrates taught that medical treatment should be scientific and not depend on magic or even religion for its success.

Aristotle, whom we have already mentioned for his theories about the universe, was extremely interested in the study of animals and plants. He found out a great deal about the anatomy of animals.

Although Aristotle was also interested in plant life, it was his friend, Theophrastus, who made the most progress in this field of science. He examined the ways in which plants begin to grow and develop, and produced the first complete book on botany.

The Ancient Greeks thus made much progress in the study of the universe, of the animal kingdom and of nature. Their efforts must be marvelled at when we remember that all this took place around the fourth and fifth centuries before Christ.

On the island of Cos, under a plane tree, young doctors took the 'Hippocratic Oath' as long ago as the 5th century BC

**Hippocrates
460 - 370 BC**

Ancient Greek stone carvings of surgical instruments

Science moves to Alexandria

During the fourth century BC, Alexander the Great conquered nearly all the countries of the Middle East. In 332 BC he built a seaport at Alexandria, on the Mediterranean coast of Egypt, and it was here that scientific thought was further developed for the next three-hundred years or so. To Alexandria came many learned men whose names are famous today. Among them Euclid, Archimedes and Ptolemy are perhaps the best known. Their ideas covered the sciences of medicine, mathematics, astronomy and geography.

In medicine, a man named Herophilus was outstanding at this time. Some of the medical terms he invented are still in use today. He made a detailed study of the human body, discovered how the human eye works and how the optic nerves are connected to the brain. From his experiments with animals (and, it is believed, with condemned criminals as well), he was able to understand the working of the lungs and the differences between arteries and veins. He also discovered the separate functions of the nerves – those which enable the body to move and those which control the senses such as touch, taste and smell.

Herophilus considered that the brain and not the heart controlled the working of the body – a belief completely opposite to that previously held.

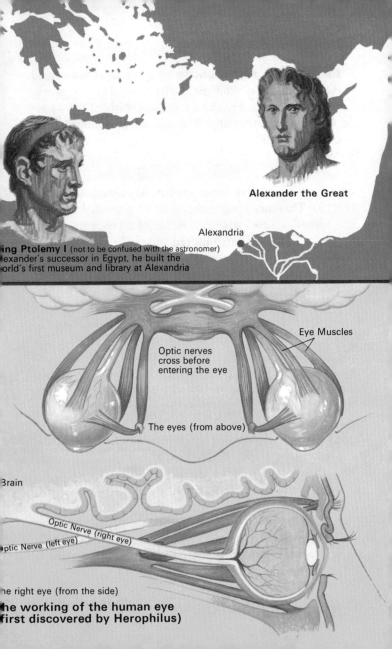

Alexander the Great

Alexandria

ing Ptolemy I (not to be confused with the astronomer)
lexander's successor in Egypt, he built the
orld's first museum and library at Alexandria

Eye Muscles

Optic nerves
cross before
entering the eye

The eyes (from above)

Brain

Optic Nerve (right eye)

ptic Nerve (left eye)

he right eye (from the side)

**he working of the human eye
first discovered by Herophilus)**

Euclid and Archimedes

Euclid was a mathematician of great fame who lived between 330 and 260 BC. His best known work, *Elements of Geometry*, was a complete study of the whole of Greek geometry, and it remained a standard text-book on the subject even until the present century.

Archimedes was also a mathematician but he was an inventor as well. He invented the Archimedean Screw (Fig. 3). This was a water-screw which provided a simple method of raising water and was used all over the world for more than fifteen hundred years. In science he is best known for his principle that a body placed in a fluid loses as much of its weight as is equal to the weight of the displaced fluid (Fig. 2).

The discovery followed a problem put to him by the ruler of Sicily. He had a new gold crown and he suspected that his jeweller had tricked him by mixing some silver with the gold. Archimedes was asked to prove this without damaging the crown. For a long time he had no success. Then, while taking a bath he realised that the water level rose as his body went under and also that his body seemed to lose weight. He realised the problem was solved, and he is said to have rushed naked through the streets of Syracuse shouting "Eureka! Eureka!" (I have found out! I have found out!).

He had found a way of comparing the density of solids by putting them in water. Thus the weight of a gold crown in water would be different from that of one made of gold and silver.

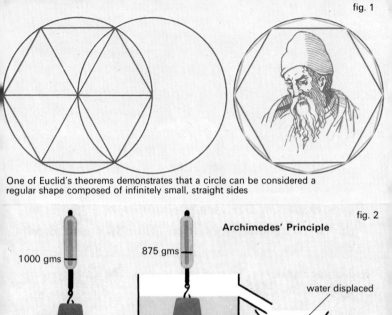

fig. 1

One of Euclid's theorems demonstrates that a circle can be considered a regular shape composed of infinitely small, straight sides

fig. 2

Archimedes' Principle

1000 gms

1000 gms

875 gms

water displaced

Upthrust 125 gms

125 gms

fig. 3

Archimedean Screw

Measuring the world

As early as 200 BC the size of the earth could be calculated with surprising accuracy. It was Eratosthenes, a pupil of Archimedes, who found a way of doing it.

Almost due south of Alexandria was a place called Syene (now Aswan). Here there was a well down which no shadow was cast when the mid-day sun was directly overhead. Using a *gnomon* he measured the angle of the sun at Alexandria when it was directly overhead at Syene. From this he was able to obtain the difference in latitude between the two places. Next, he employed a *pacer* – a man who was trained to pace out distances by walking in steps of equal length, counting as he went. In this way the distance between Alexandria and Syene was measured.

With this information Eratosthenes was able to work out the circumference of the earth (see the diagram opposite). Considering the primitive methods used, his measurement of 24,000 miles (38 624km) was amazingly close to the figure accepted today of 24,800 miles (39 911km).

Thus, as long ago as two hundred years before the birth of Christ, Man had a very good idea of the size of the world he lived in.

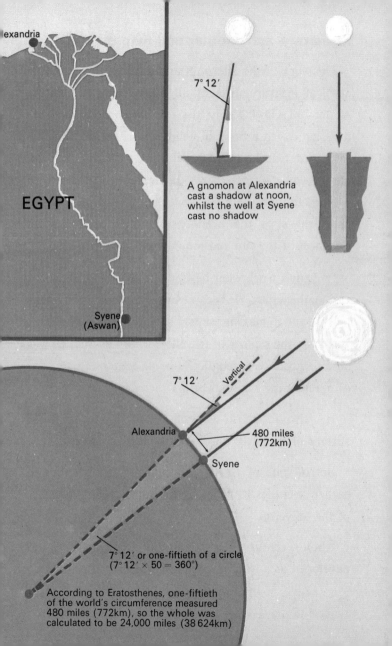

Alexandria

EGYPT

Syene
(Aswan)

7° 12'

A gnomon at Alexandria
cast a shadow at noon,
whilst the well at Syene
cast no shadow

7° 12'

Vertical

Alexandria

480 miles
(772km)

Syene

7° 12' or one-fiftieth of a circle
(7° 12' × 50 = 360°)

According to Eratosthenes, one-fiftieth
of the world's circumference measured
480 miles (772km), so the whole was
calculated to be 24,000 miles (38 624km)

Ptolemy – astronomer and map maker

The work of the Alexandrians continued, with astronomical measurements of all kinds being calculated. About 150 AD, Ptolemy, the greatest astronomer of his time, produced a book in which he collected all the information then known, as well as his own observations. He gave in detail the sizes of the sun and moon and what he thought were the movements of the planets. He listed the stars that were visible and dealt with the distances of the sun and moon from the earth.

Ptolemy's work went beyond the study of astronomy and mathematics. He became interested in the behaviour of light and in making maps. From his own observations and from the reports of travellers whom he met, he was able to produce a geography book containing an atlas of maps of the known world.

He also found a way of illustrating the rounded surface of the earth on the flat surface of a book.

But in spite of all his knowledge, Ptolemy followed earlier scientists in believing the earth to be the centre of the universe.

About a century after the time of Ptolemy, algebra was developed as a way of solving mathematical problems.

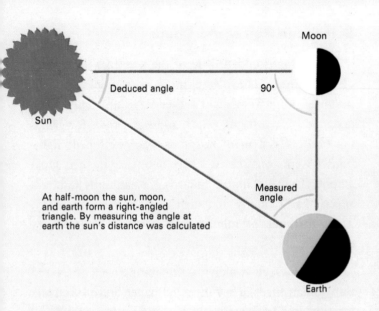

Sun

Deduced angle

90°

Moon

At half-moon the sun, moon, and earth form a right-angled triangle. By measuring the angle at earth the sun's distance was calculated

Measured angle

Earth

The World according to Ptolemy

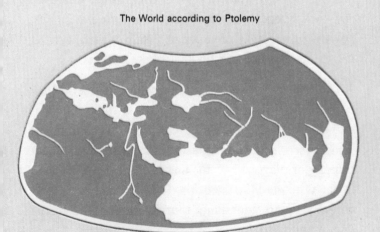

Science in Rome and China

The Romans added little to the scientific knowledge of their time. They were more concerned with the practical improvements to everyday life. They built aqueducts for carrying water, and water mills for grinding corn; a system of hospitals was developed; lighthouses were constructed where necessary in their great empire. They had high standards of cleanliness and built special baths, many of which can still be seen today. Their methods of mining and smelting became very efficient.

The Chinese have a civilisation dating back at least to Babylonian times. They invented paper, introduced silk farming on a large scale and started printing from wood blocks. They were interested in astronomy, but used their knowledge to try to foretell the future, a system now called astrology. If you read certain newspapers and magazines you will still find astrology sections.

The Ancient Chinese were interested in numbers. They evolved the 'Magic Square', which is a square divided into smaller squares, each of which contains a number. Whichever way the numbers are added – vertically, horizontally or diagonally – the answer is always the same. In the example illustrated, the four corner figures, and also any square containing four figures, add up to the same total.

Roman Bridge and Aqueduct

3,000 mile long Great Wall of China, built 200 BC

15	10	8	1
6	3	13	12
9	16	2	7
4	5	11	14

Chemistry

For very many centuries chemistry – or alchemy as it was then called – was thought to be a weird and mysterious subject. Alchemy originated about 100 AD in Alexandria and continued for another fifteen centuries before the beginnings of modern chemistry.

The alchemists believed that one metal could be changed into another and they were always looking for a magical formula which would turn ordinary metals into gold. They were also in search of a potion which would cure all ills. Fruitless though the search was, new chemical processes were discovered, such as distillation, which were to help chemists centuries later.

At about the 8th century, the Arabs carried on the work of the Greeks, and although they made few great discoveries in chemistry, perhaps their careful records were their great contribution. Knowledge and ideas spread very slowly at that time and much valuable information was never passed on at all. Without the records made by the Arabs, it is possible that most of Greek scientific thought might have disappeared or at least been lost for a very long time.

These 16th century woodcuts show two quite different laboratory activities of the time. The muddle of the alchemist's laboratory (above) contrasts with the chemical laboratory (below) where gold and silver are being separated.

Science reaches the West

Very few more new scientific facts were discovered for a period of several hundred years. Sometimes accepted theories were abandoned and some people even went back to believing that the earth was flat. The Christian Church at that time did not encourage too much scientific progress; science was not regarded as having anything to do with the preaching of the Gospel or with the saving of souls. However, a few Christians, St. Augustine of Hippo among them, did collect together some of the known scientific facts and translated several of the early books into Latin.

It was during the twelfth century that science moved forward again. This time the centre of learning was the city of Toledo in Spain. Here gathered a new generation of scholars of many nationalities, and they translated the original Greek writings so that the work of the earlier scientists became more widely known.

Suddenly the scene changed. People thought up new ideas; new theories and explanations were offered to account for the wonders of the universe. Technology also went ahead as scientific thought was applied to machines and instruments. Manufacturers tried to find better ways of making things; water power was introduced into a greater number of industries and wooden gear-wheels were developed to help drive many kinds of machinery.

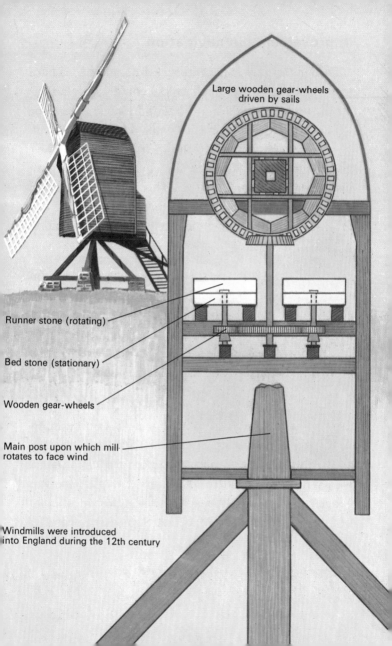

Large wooden gear-wheels
driven by sails

Runner stone (rotating)

Bed stone (stationary)

Wooden gear-wheels

Main post upon which mill
rotates to face wind

Windmills were introduced
into England during the 12th century

Improvements in navigation

During the thirteenth century, astronomers tried hard to find a method by which sailors could navigate their way across the seas using the stars to guide them. The introduction of the magnetic compass was a great help. Mariners were also able to fix their latitude (i.e., their position north or south of the equator), by using an instrument called an *astrolabe*. This instrument enabled them to work out the height of the stars in the sky. But they were not able to find their longitude – their position east or west.

The problem was not solved completely until the invention of the marine chronometer in the eighteenth century, but considerable progress had been made by the fifteenth century.* The stars, sun and moon could be observed with reasonable accuracy, and a ship's position plotted and course set by using mathematics.

When Christopher Columbus sailed across the Atlantic, in 1492, he might have wished for a little more information to help him navigate, but his successful voyages showed what great advances had been made, and other men were encouraged to follow his example. One was Magellan who, in 1520, reached the southernmost point of South America. The Magellan Strait is named after him.

* *See the Ladybird book 'Time, Calendars and Clocks'.*

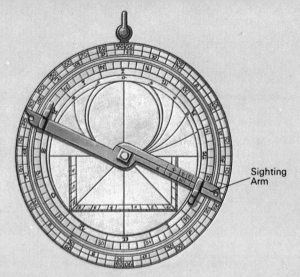

The astrolabe was suspended by a chord through a ring at the top and a star sighted along the rotating arm. The star's angle of elevation was then read off the scale

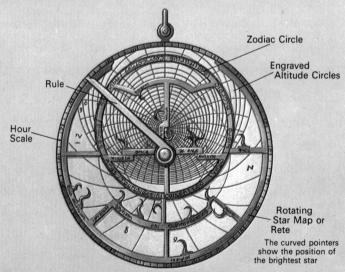

Zodiac Circle

Engraved Altitude Circles

Rule

Hour Scale

Sighting Arm

Rotating Star Map or Rete

The curved pointers show the position of the brightest star

The other side of the astrolabe could be used for telling the time. The rete was rotated until the pointer for the sighted star lay on the correct circle of altitude and the rule lined up with the sun's position on the zodiac circle. The rule's pointer then gave the correct time on the hour scale

A changing world

With improved navigation the way was now open for other explorers and navigators to cross the seas in search of new adventures and new lands. On their return they told exciting tales of different peoples, new kinds of animals and plants, and a variety of minerals hitherto unheard of in their own countries. By the end of the 16th century, the known area of the world was twice as great as that known to the Greeks at the time of Ptolemy.

Sometime between 1440 and 1450 came an invention that was to revolutionise the spreading of knowledge throughout the civilised world. This was the invention of printing by movable type. The inventor was a German named Johann Gutenberg. His new method was much cheaper, easier and quicker than the old way of carving whole pages from blocks of wood.*

During the following hundred years or so there was much scientific activity in many countries of the western world. Plants, animals and marine life were all studied in detail, and the new facts were published in numerous printed books which were produced in Germany, England, France, Holland, Switzerland and Italy.

* See the Ladybird book 'The Story of Printing'.

An early printing machine using movable type.

Leonardo da Vinci

Before we leave what is known as the Renaissance period in Europe, something should be said about a man of outstanding genius – Leonardo da Vinci. Surprisingly, he had very little influence on the science of his time and his work became fully appreciated only after his death, when his notebooks were deciphered.

Leonardo da Vinci (1452–1519) was an Italian painter, sculptor, architect, scientist, engineer and musician! He believed that science could progress only through observation and experiment. As an artist, he wanted to draw the human body with more realism than had previously been possible, so he made a detailed study of its bone structure and muscles. Not content with this, he dissected a number of dead bodies and made drawings of veins and arteries as well as most of the internal organs.

As a scientist, Leonardo da Vinci studied *hydrodynamics* – the flow of water through channels and the formation of waves. He introduced the idea of air waves and established the laws of sound. He investigated the properties of light and realised the possibility of light waves. He believed that the earth was not the centre of the universe but a star like all the other stars.

opposite :
Sketches from Leonardo da Vinci's notebook

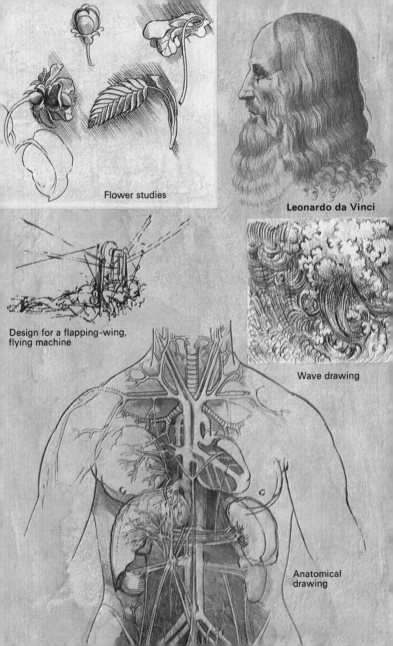

Flower studies

Leonardo da Vinci

Design for a flapping-wing, flying machine

Wave drawing

Anatomical drawing

The new astronomy

In spite of all the new thinking, many branches of science still relied on the centuries-old theories of the Greek philosophers. This was particularly true of astronomy.

The first person seriously to question the ideas of Aristotle and Ptolemy was a man named Copernicus (1473–1543). He is said to be the founder of modern astronomy. He believed the sun to be the centre of the universe. Unfortunately, the book in which he set out to prove this theory could be published only at the time of his death, for fear of the trouble his revolutionary ideas would stir up.

The next person to produce new ideas on astronomy was Tycho Brahe, a Danish nobleman's son, who set up an observatory on the island of Hveen, near Copenhagen. There, for over twenty years, he carried out accurate observations of the heavenly bodies, and compiled detailed tables of their movements. His instruments were mainly quadrants and sextants which he designed himself. He realised that no equipment could be completely accurate, so when he conducted his observations he made allowances for the error in each of his instruments. This principle has been adopted by scientists ever since.

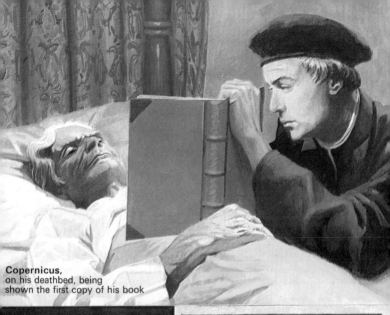

Copernicus,
on his deathbed, being
shown the first copy of his book

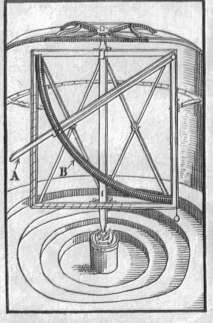

Tycho Brahe and an engraving
of a quadrant from one of his books
published in 1602.
A star was sighted along the arm A
and its angle read off from the
quadrant B, which had a radius of
over 6′ (1.8m) and was calibrated in
fractions of a degree

Changing ideas on the universe

The idea that the sun, not the earth, was the centre of the universe took a great number of years to be accepted. The Churches of Europe, especially, did not want change of any kind. They preferred to rely on the old theories which better suited their beliefs. Nevertheless, through the work of Copernicus, Tycho Brahe and others, the idea gradually took root. It was Johann Kepler, a German, who provided further evidence and discovered the true paths of the planets. He believed also that God had some special purpose in making the universe the way it was.

For about 14 years Kepler was assistant to Tycho Brahe, whose measurements he was able to use in working out his own laws of planetary motion. After five years of studying the paths of planets he found that their orbits around the sun are oval, or elliptical, in shape (Fig. 1).

He also found that the nearer a planet is to the sun during its orbit the faster it moves, so that its average speed depends upon its distance from the sun (Fig. 2).

Kepler's conclusions upset all previous ideas on the subject; since the days of Pythagoras and Aristotle planets had been thought to move in circles and at a constant speed.

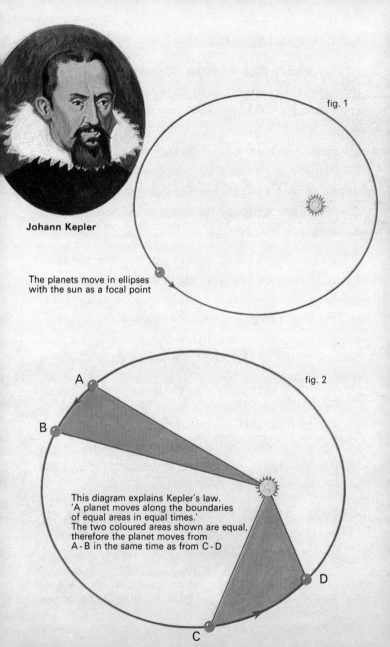

Johann Kepler

The planets move in ellipses
with the sun as a focal point

fig. 1

fig. 2

A

B

This diagram explains Kepler's law.
'A planet moves along the boundaries
of equal areas in equal times.'
The two coloured areas shown are equal,
therefore the planet moves from
A - B in the same time as from C - D

D

C

Galileo and the telescope

The great Italian scientist, Galileo, lived at about the same time as Kepler. In 1609 he heard of a Dutch spectacle-maker's invention of the telescope, an instrument which had two lenses separated from one another at opposite ends of a tube. Galileo made a telescope of his own and improved it until he could greatly magnify distant objects. Galileo, therefore, is given the credit for the invention which opened up vast new possibilities in astronomy.

Galileo himself made several important discoveries. Using his telescope he was able to see the mountains on the moon, spots on the sun, the four satellites of Jupiter and the ring of Saturn. He proved finally that the theories of the early Greek scientists were incorrect. The mountainous nature of the moon, for instance, showed that it was of similar substances to the earth.

Yet, despite all the evidence that Galileo was able to present, there were those in authority who were still unwilling to change their long-held beliefs. Galileo was tried by the Inquisition, placed under arrest and forced to deny the truth of some of his own discoveries.

In Book 2 we shall see how science progressed into modern times, often in spite of dispute and disbelief.

Above: Galileo made his own telescope.
Below: A Dutch boy and his father chance upon the principle of the telescope.

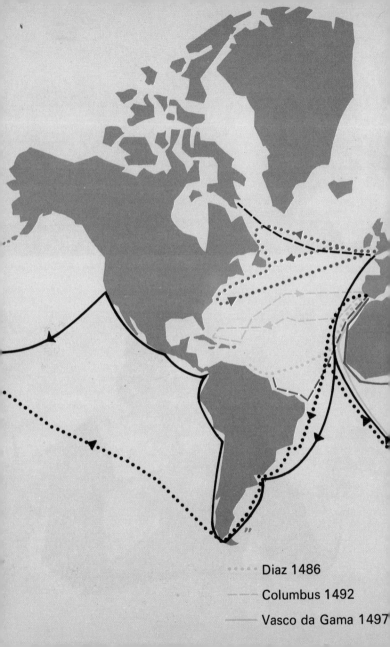

..... Diaz 1486
- - - Columbus 1492
——— Vasco da Gama 1497